Peaceful Hippo

Written by Judy Nayer

Celebration Press

Parsippany, New Jersey

Table of Contents

Hippos in the Water 4

Hippos on Land 8

Hippos in Families and Groups 10

Hippos in the Future 15

The hippopotamus is the third-largest animal on land. The only land animals larger than the hippo are the elephant and the white rhinoceros.

The name *hippopotamus* means "river horse." But hippos are more like pigs than horses. Pigs and hippos both have very round bodies. They both love mud. Their eyes, ears, and feet are similar, too.

Common Hippopotamus

Size: Up to 13 feet long and 5 feet tall

Weight: Up to 4 tons (8,000 pounds)

Hippos in the Water

Hippos live in rivers, lakes, or swamps. They spend most of their time in the water. During the day, hippos hide, sleep, and rest in the water. They move by swimming or by walking along the bottoms of rivers or lakes.

Hippos like the water because it makes it easier for them to move. They don't have to work as hard to stand up. Hippos can't float, though. Their bodies are too massive. Sometimes hippos dive underwater to rest. They can stay underwater for up to six minutes.

Hippos also stay in the water to keep cool. The water keeps their skin from burning and drying out in the hot sun.

Hippos' eyes, ears, and nostrils are at the tops of their heads. This lets them see, hear, and breathe while they're mostly underwater.

Hippos on Land

Every night, hippos come out of the water to look for food. Hippos are plant-eating animals. They eat mostly grass. They can eat 100 pounds of grass each night! Before morning the hippos are back in the water.

With their huge, barrel-shaped bodies and
short legs, hippos don't look like fast runners,
but they are. Hippos can gallop along at 40
miles per hour! The ground shakes as they run.

Hippos in Families and Groups

Hippos live in groups of 10, 20, or even 100. The females and young hippos stay together in a nursery. The male hippos stay around the edge of the nursery. Each male claims his own space to live, called his territory.

Hippos are mostly peaceful, but sometimes male hippos fight each other. This happens when one male comes too close to another's territory. The hippo opens its mouth very wide and shows its teeth. These teeth are huge. The biggest ones are 28 inches long!

Sometimes the hippo opens its huge mouth and makes a sound like a person laughing. People who study hippos think this sound may be a warning to another hippo.

A mother hippo has a new baby every year. It's a big baby—about 100 pounds—but that is small compared with its mother! A baby hippo often rides on its mother's back.

A hippo is not fully grown until it is four years old. Until then it stays very close to its mother. She must protect it from animals like lions and crocodiles. When a mother goes up on land for food, the other hippo mothers "baby-sit" until she comes back.

Hippos in the Future

Adult hippos have only one enemy—people. People have hunted hippos for their hides, meat, and ivory teeth. Hippos have lost their homes as people have taken over their land.

Once hippos lived in different parts of the world. Today they live only in parts of Africa.

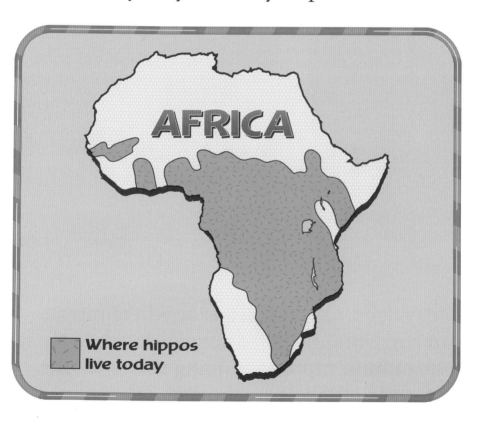

Where hippos live today

Today, land has been set aside where hippos can live without fear of being hunted. In these reservations, hippos are doing very well. In fact, their numbers are growing.